Paints and materials

Charles Brady

A Chelsea College Project sponsored by the Nuffield Foundation and the Social Science Research Council

Published for Chelsea College, University of London, by Macdonald Educational, London and Milwaukee

First published in Great Britain 1976 by
Macdonald Educational Ltd
Holywell House, Worship Street
London EC2A 2EN

Macdonald-Raintree Inc
205 W. Highland Avenue
Milwaukee, Wisconsin 53203

Reprinted 1977, 1978, 1979, 1981

© Chelsea College, University of London, 1976

ISBN 0 356 05075 0

Library of Congress Catalog Card Number 77-82985

Made and printed by
Morrison & Gibb Limited, London and Edinburgh

Project team

Project organizer : John Bird

Team members :   Dorothy Diamond (full-time)
                 Keith Geary
                 Don Plimmer
                 Ed Catherall

Evaluators :   Ted Johnston
                 Tom Robertson

Editors

Penny Butler
Macdonald Educational

John Pettit
Nuffield Foundation Science Teaching Project
Publications Department

General preface

The books published under the series title Teaching Primary Science are the work of the College Curriculum Science Studies project. This project is sponsored jointly by the Nuffield Foundation and the Social Science Research Council. It aims to provide support and guidance to students who are about to teach science in primary schools.

Although the College Curriculum Science Studies materials have been produced with the student teacher very much in mind, we suggest that they will also be of use to teachers and to lecturers or advisers—in fact to anyone with an interest in primary school science. Hence this series of books.

Three main questions are considered important:

What is science?

Why teach science?

How does one teach science?

A very broad view is taken of teacher training. Training does not, and should not, stop once an in-service or college course has been completed, but can and does take place on a self-help basis in the classroom. In each context, however, we consider that it works best through the combined effects of:

1 Science Science activities studied practically at the teacher's level before use in class.

2 Children Observation of children's scientific activities and their responses to particular methods of teaching and class organization.

3 Teachers Consideration of the methods used by colleagues in the classroom.

4 Resources A study of materials useful in the teaching of science.

5 Discussion and thought A critical consideration of the *what*, the *why* and the *how* of science teaching, on the basis of these experiences. This is particularly important because we feel that there is no one way of teaching any more than there is any one totally satisfactory solution to a scientific problem. It is a question of the individual teacher having to make the 'best' choice available to him in a particular situation.

To help with this choice there are, at frequent intervals, special points to consider; these are marked by a coloured tint. We hope that they will stimulate answers to such questions as 'How did this teacher approach a teaching problem? Did it work for him? Would it work for me? What have I done in a situation like that?' In this way the reader can look critically at his own experience and share it by discussion with colleagues.

All our books reflect this five-fold pattern of experiences, although there are differences of emphasis. For example, some lay more stress on particular science topics and others on teaching methods.

In addition, there is a lecturers' guide *Students, teachers and science* which deals specifically with different methods and approaches suitable for the college or in-service course in primary science but, like the other books in the series, it should be of use to students and teachers as well as to lecturers.

Contents

Introduction

Children can get a great deal of pleasure from working with paints and materials. They have the chance to learn new skills and have something attractive to show at the end of it.

This book is not a manual on teaching art, but it does draw upon some of the materials and techniques of artistic expression to explore ways of asking questions and finding answers in a scientific way.

Each chapter contains an activity and a list of materials for practical experience. This is followed by an analysis of the activity and a consideration of work with children, which should be supplemented by direct experience in the classroom. The emphasis differs in each chapter. 'Finding ways to record on paper' is concerned with organization and objectives; 'Resist painting' involves the discussion of concepts, while 'Working with powder colour and inks' examines scientific skills.

We hope that by following the suggestions and references for further work, teachers, students and tutors can continue where this book ends.

1 Finding ways to record on paper

You will need:

Leaves and bark
Tempera powder colour
School paste or decorators' cold-water paste
Spoon
Hard rubber roller
Pencils (2B, HB and 2H)
Rubber
Coloured chalks
Wax crayons
Paper (cheaper-grade drawing paper or lining paper)
Water
Flat tray or dish
Paint brushes

Trying it yourself

Here, as in the following chapters, we advise you to try the activities before doing them with the children.

Drawing and painting   Draw and paint an accurate record of a leaf and some tree bark.

Prints and rubbings
Prints   Experiment to make a suitable printing 'ink' by mixing small amounts of powder colour, paste and water to a creamy consistency in a tray.

Use the roller or a brush to apply a film of this 'ink' to the leaf or bark.

Press the inked leaf or bark against the paper.

Rubbings   Lay the paper against the leaf or bark and rub the back of the paper with a crayon or pencil.

Prints from leaves which were 'inked' using a roller

Finding ways to make leaf rubbings using crayon, pencil and chalk

Try combining these techniques. Remember, you are trying to make an accurate record. You may find it helpful to note the material and technique used at each stage of your investigation.

You can make prints and rubbings from many kinds of surface, for instance:

Ironwork
Brasswork

Stonework from churchyards
Embossed glass
Fabrics
Paper cut-outs
Wood
Stone

All these provide magnificent scope for recording techniques.

Taking a rubbing of a manhole cover with a wax crayon (Permission should be obtained before taking rubbings in churches.)

Materials   Explore the effect of 'inks' and paints not only on paper of different absorbencies and colour but also on materials of different textures. Here are some you might try:

Cardboard	Canvas
Corrugated board	Hessian
Sandpaper	Baking foil
Cotton	Polythene
Expanded polystyrene	Wood

You could also try taking rubbings with some of these materials.

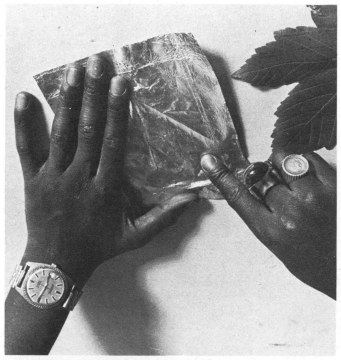

Using baking foil to make a leaf impression by rubbing

Paper   Treat paper in various ways:

Crumpled and then smoothed.
Soaked in water and dried.
Rubbed with turpentine substitute.
Smeared with petroleum jelly.

Then paint the treated papers.

Analysing your work

In making prints and taking rubbings you have been involved in a number of processes. How far you went will have varied according to your motivation, experience and existing skills.

Here is a list of processes. To what extent were you involved in them?

1   Putting ideas to the test before accepting or rejecting them.

2   Learning about the properties of drawing and painting materials.

3   Acquiring new skills such as using a roller to apply inks.

4   Working systematically by changing one variable at a time.

In analysing your work it may help to consider how Tim and Gillian, aged eight, set about doing some leaf prints.

5

Tim's and Gillian's leaf prints

The teacher started by showing the children a fairly successful set of leaf prints that had been done before. This gave them some idea of what was needed, and the kind of standard required. Rather than tell the children the best technique the teacher encouraged them to experiment for themselves. Mainly this was by *setting standards* and *suggesting alternative approaches*, saying in effect 'I wonder if you can make this picture better; why not try . . . ?'

Between them they decided that they would try to produce prints in black powder paint. Tim, who had never done prints before, but *had* done rubbings, started by putting the leaf under the paper and applying

a wash to the other side. He was soon put right by Gillian.

Throughout, their general method was to apply the paint-covered surface *directly* to the paper. At first both children used a roller, but soon discarded this in favour of hand pressing, which they found produced just as good an effect. One of the main problems was the thinness of the paint. Gillian tried to overcome this by successively:

Varying the amount of paint brushed onto the leaf.

Making several prints with a leaf after only one application of paint.

Trying to take off some of the excess paint by pressing the leaf first on a piece of newspaper.

Tim's and Gillian's early experiments

When none of these methods worked it was decided to make the paint thicker. So the teacher suggested adding some Polyfilla rather than putting in more powder. At the same time the children decided that the prints should be done on blotting paper instead of drawing paper.

Once Tim and Gillian had learnt how much paint to apply to the leaf the improvement was dramatic. They also found that leaves with more prominent veins produced a different and perhaps more striking effect. Now they were more easily able to predict which methods would produce the more accurate results, so they used some leaf prints to make a simple design.

Good print resulting from Tim's and Gillian's research and development

Changing one variable at a time In general they tested one alternative at a time. This was the most informative and helpful type of test because they then knew that it was this alternative and none other that produced a particular result. Where two alternatives were tried simultaneously (as with the blotting paper and the type of paint) this was less informative but still more useful than a completely haphazard process.

Which other processes listed on page 5 did Tim and Gillian follow?

Children recording on paper

The interest of the children might arise in two ways:

The thrill of testing new methods and materials *for their own sake*.

The need to produce a satisfying aesthetic effect.

But it might also come about because the recording serves much broader purposes, for instance:

Making and keeping records of embossed bottles, manhole and drain covers (see page 13 top and Chapter 2).

Historical records of stonework and brasswork in churches (see page 14 left).

Comparing the brick and stonework of different buildings.

Comparing different types of wood and trees.

See bibliography: 2, 3, 6, 9.

The mechanics of class organization

The children's work requires careful organization, and this we can consider under two broad headings: organizing for scientific objectives (see page 10) and the mechanics of class organization.

In organizing group work you may need to decide the following issues.

Grouping   How many groups will be involved? How large will each group be?

Materials   Have you sufficient materials and spares? For example, for recording on paper a group of four children can usually work effectively with:

Small tin lid of powder colour and a spoon
Plastic yoghurt carton half filled with paste, and another spoon
Four sticks of chalk and four crayons
Four trays or dishes and a roller
One pencil of each grade
Single sheet of paper cut to about A4 size (each child has his own sheet)

Position   Where should the groups be placed? Bear in mind, in particular, the need for:

Easy access to resources and services.
Avoiding unnecessary traffic through the classroom.

Furniture   Do you have to reorganize the furniture?

Speed and sequence   When the children are using many different methods, will some children finish more quickly than others? What will the children do when they have finished?

Mess   How will you prevent the children making an unnecessary mess of themselves and the classroom?

What will the rest do?   If only some of the class are involved, what will the others be doing at the same time? For example, a junior teacher writes: 'The activity was organized by having the rest of the class working on activities that did not require my continual attention. For example, while I worked with this group of four, some children were making Plasticine models, some worked on their own topic books (pictures, drawing, writing), on maths not needing help and on private study (reading).'

Supervision   Could one or more groups work outside the main group without supervision? With a class of, say, thirty-two children in groups of four, consider these choices:

The whole class is engaged in this activity simultaneously, but shares the materials which are in a central pool.

One group of four carries out the investigations you made (described at the beginning of the chapter), while other groups work at something else such as project work, painting, reading, or another investigation.

Two groups of four carry out the investigations as part of a class theme or topic (for example, 'Trees').

Desks are moved to make four large tables, each of which will accommodate eight pupils. The basic activity is divided into four investigations and appropriate material for one investigation is placed on one table, for another investigation on another table, and so on. Children may move from table to table when you and they agree.

How might you break up the activity into four convenient units?

Each method of organization has problems. What snags do you find with your methods?

Some sample problems

Next is a short account of the work of three students with groups of children. If you were asked to offer them some advice what would you say? What are the possible reasons for their lack of success?

Student A, working with a small class of ten-year-olds, distributed the materials and said 'Find the best ways to record leaves and bark.' After ten minutes the lesson was abandoned. Later the student was overheard muttering 'Never, oh never, again. . . .'

Student B, working with seven-year-olds, decided to make a 'nature' folder for them. She enjoyed working in her flat decorating the folder with leaf prints and bark rubbings. When she presented the folder to the children, they did not seem to be very interested in her work, but they enjoyed cutting from magazines pictures of trees to put inside the folder.

Student C, working with a class of six-year-olds, had organized the children into small groups engaged in number activities. One group was working with coins. After a while she noticed that the children in this group had discovered the technique of using paper and pencil to take rubbings of coins, and seemed to be quite excited by this. She reprimanded the group and took the pencils, paper and coins from the children.

Organizing for scientific objectives

You *can* just tell or show children what to do. For example, if you demonstrate how to use a paint roller for applying paint and ask children to paint a picture with the roller, they will learn something about the properties of rolled paint and may acquire a new skill.

On the other hand, you can sometimes also enrich a child's experience by encouraging him or her to work systematically and critically (see page 12).

Refer to the analysis of your own work and then consider how the work described below encourages children to test ideas before accepting or rejecting them, and to work systematically by changing one variable at a time.

Note how difficult it is to hold many variables in mind at one time. The ability to manipulate these variables is a scientific skill which children only seem to acquire when they are able to think in the abstract. You will probably find that most children in primary schools can only

consider one pair of alternatives at a time, but look out for the gifted child.

Some examples

1 Children aged ten, preparing for an excursion to a park to study the living environment, are being briefed before setting out. They know how to take bark rubbings and some children want to do this. One girl, however, would like to identify the trees instead. The teacher combines the tree-spotting group which has an identification book, with the bark-rubbing group which has crayons and paper, and suggests that it is possible to identify trees from their bark pattern.

2 The teacher has brought to school some chestnut leaves for her class of seven-year-olds.

Jonathan: 'Can I draw them, Miss?'
Teacher: 'Yes, here's some paper.'
Jonathan: 'Can I use crayons, Miss?'
Teacher: 'Yes, but you might like to try pencil.'
Abigail: 'I want to use pencil.'
Jonathan: 'Can I draw round the leaf, Miss?'
Abigail: 'I want to draw round the leaf.'
Teacher: 'Let's see which looks most like the leaf, the crayon drawing or the pencil drawing. When we have done that, I'll show you another way. Then we can compare all three.'
Jonathan: 'Can we try with other leaves too?'

3 Over a number of sessions with eleven-year-olds doing recording, the teacher was concerned not so much with the pupils' final results as with the extent of their investigations. He encouraged careful note-taking and, as he moved among the pupils, he suggested various alternatives for them to try. After the pupils had cleared the materials away, there was always some time reserved for a display and discussion of the work.

The school enjoyed a high reputation for the quality of its art work.

Make a note of what happens with your own pupils.

Collect samples of pupils' work for exhibition and discussion.

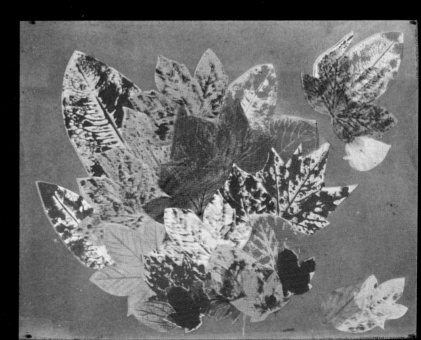

Leaf prints and rubbings arranged as a montage for
classroom display (see Chapter 1)

Nadine.

Nadine's paint was 'too wet'

Illustration 6

Darren

Darren's paint was thick.

Nadine's and Darren's leaf prints, showing that individual experimental results can be of use to the whole class (see page 10)

Wax-crayon resist and colour wash of manhole
covers (see pages 8, 18)

Yellow wax-crayon resist and mauve colour wash
design from a grille (see pages 8, 18)

Below: Brass rubbing from a church (see page 4)
Permission should be obtained before taking rubbings in churches.

Above: Spatter painting (see page 24)

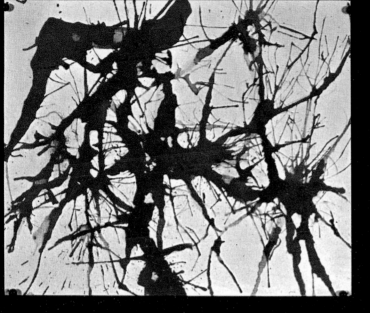

Drop and puff painting (see page 24)

Frayed string dipped in paint and pressed in a
folded sheet of paper (see page 24)

Above: A montage produced from separating mixtures of food colourings (see pages 26-27)

Below: Experimenting with tints (see page 26)

Tints from adding white.

These are my red and white mixtures I liked the palest pink best

I made these pretty colours from purples and white my little girl has a purple maxi

2 Resist painting

You will need:

White and coloured paper and card
Liquid or powder tempera colour
Wax crayons and candles
Liquid floor or furniture wax and a dropper
Wide brushes

Food colouring and water-soluble inks
Water and containers such as discarded yoghurt pots, baking tins, etc
Quick-drying household waterproof adhesive, for example Dufix or Bostic Clear
Cocktail or other pointed sticks
Sugar paper, blotting paper, lining paper

Applying a wash to a candle-wax resist taken from manhole covers

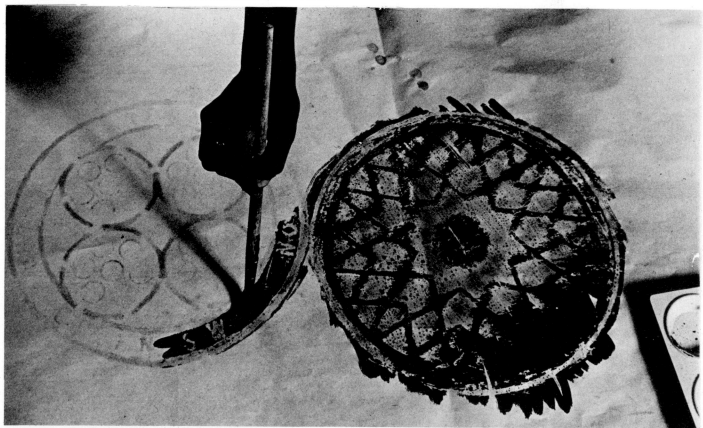

Trying it yourself

The principle of resist painting is that water and resistant substances (resists) do not mix.

Make a design on paper with one of the wax resists listed (page 17). You can then paint over this with water-soluble paint, ink, or dye, which soaks into the paper in the spaces not covered by the resist (see page 13).

Try the following, with variants and combinations as you wish. As you proceed, you may find it helpful to note the techniques, for later reference.

Using a white wax candle to make a resist design

1 Draw a design on white or coloured paper with a wax candle, coloured crayon or liquid floor wax. If you use liquid wax, allow it a few minutes to dry. Apply a colour wash using a broad brush.

2 Cover a surface with powder colour. Let it dry and then apply a design using any resist. When this is dry wash the surface under clean water.

3 Cover a surface with wax. Scratch a design and flood with colour wash.

4 Scratch a design into glazed card, and flood with colour wash.

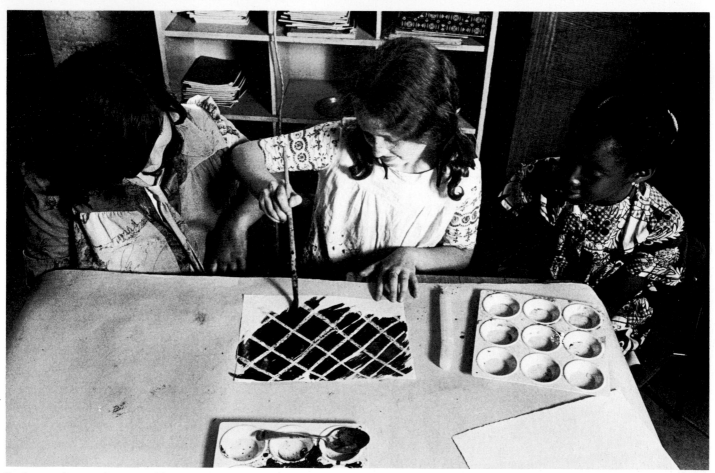
Putting a colour wash over a white wax candle resist

More resist painting

Try the following. You can use the same materials as for the basic activity of resist painting.

5   Put a few drops of water onto some sugar paper, blotting paper or lining paper and watch what happens. Rub a second piece of the same kind of paper thoroughly with a wax crayon or candle. Put a few drops of water on this surface. What differences do you observe? Now apply a colour wash to each surface. What happens and how would you explain what you observe?

6   Paint a piece of paper with tempera colour and allow it to dry. Rub half of the painted surface with wax.

Immerse the whole piece of paper in water.

7   By experimenting, find whether or not tempera colour can be used as a transparent wash as well as an opaque medium.

8   By testing the media available, prepare two lists:

Substances which mix together.
Substances which do not mix together.

Would you organize any of the activities nos 5–8 before, during, or after nos 1–4 (page 18)? For example, you might say that no. 5 should come first because it introduces children clearly to the idea that resists repel water.

Extending resist technique

1 Pin cotton over a pad of newspapers onto a table top. Apply designs with flour-and-water paste. When the paste dries apply Dylon dye mixed with Paintex thickener and cold dye fix. When dry, wash out the paste.

2 Put white oil-based printer's ink on cardboard shapes and print them on white paper. Superimpose a print of a similar shape from another piece of cardboard inked with water-soluble ink.

3 Paint a shape with white tempera on white paper. When dry, brush waterproof ink all over the paper. When this dries, gently scrub the paper under a running tap.

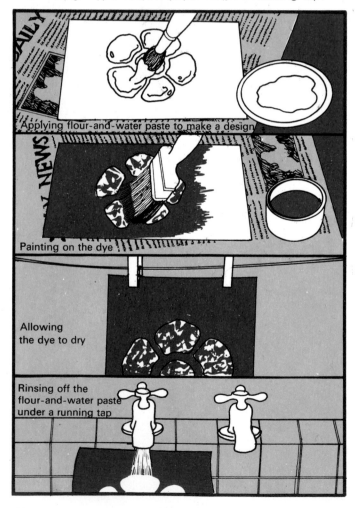

Applying flour-and-water paste to make a design

Painting on the dye

Allowing the dye to dry

Rinsing off the flour-and-water paste under a running tap

Analysing your work

Understanding resist painting involves concepts. Concepts are generalized ideas which a person can have without reference to specific examples. For instance, you may form a concept of a liquid as anything that flows, without having to refer to water, milk, etc. But to form the concept of a generalized liquid, one needs experience of many liquids. Gradually the characteristic properties of liquids can be understood without reference to examples.

Here is a list of concepts associated with this chapter's activities. When you were doing resist painting, which concepts were you involved with? Were there others?

Absorption	Wetness
Repelling	Dryness
Dissolving	Mixing
Solubility	Transparency
Insolubility	Opacity
Liquid	Porosity
Solid	Impermeability

Can you add to the list?

Trying it with children: words and concepts

Children making resist paintings will be involved with the same concepts as you were. The essential difference between your involvement and that of the children might be that because of your age and experience you can order and analyse processes much more than young children can.

Concept formation in children is a gradual process. While there is much that is not known about it, it is generally accepted that the process depends on the children's first-hand experience and that language plays an important part in ordering that experience.

How might you use words to reinforce the experience of children doing resist painting? One way is for you, the teacher, to provide new words for the children.

However, as James Britton says, 'It is from successive experience of words in use—words used for some actual profit or pleasure—that a child builds up his resources.'

See bibliography: 14.

In *The Language of Primary School Children* Cónnie and Harold Rosen put another point of view:

'Children have available much more linguistic competence than usually finds its way into their speech. We need then to create those situations which exert the greatest pressure on them to use their latent resources. . . . [We are] profoundly disturbed by [our] experience of children being given their ration of good (better? best?) words to cope with . . . what?'

See bibliography: 15.

Methods
Consider these methods of introducing vocabulary to children:

1   The teacher puts the key words onto the blackboard. The pupils are asked to copy and say them.

2   The teacher uses words relating to the process involved, say 'design' or 'pattern'. The words vary but the teacher introduces them deliberately.

3   Individual children are asked to describe to the group or to the teacher exactly what was done to obtain a particular effect.

4   When children obtain a really interesting or dramatic effect, they are asked to suggest what it means to them.

Which of these work for you?

Conversation with children

These are some extracts from conversations with children doing resist painting. Would it help if the teacher were to introduce new words?

Kirsten and Paul (aged ten) are putting some liquid furniture polish on paper.

Kirsten: 'Look, you can see the writing on that newspaper underneath.'
Paul: 'Oh, yeah!'
Teacher: 'What's a word that means that things can be seen through?'
Paul: 'Ummm . . . easy?'
Kirsten: 'Er : . . see through it?'

Kirsten has put drops of water on the waxed and unwaxed sides of a piece of paper.

Teacher: 'What's happening, Kirsten?'
Kirsten: 'Well, on the side without the wax it's sort of soaking in, and on the other side it's bubbly.'
Paul: 'It's stopping on the top.'
Kirsten: 'Yes, it's not letting it through.'
(Kirsten holds the paper at an angle and the drops roll off.)
Kirsten: 'On this side it runs and on the other side it doesn't.'
Teacher: 'Why?'
Paul: 'Because the wax is skiddy.'
Teacher: 'What do you mean?'
Paul: 'When the candle's burning in the power cut it runs down the side really fast. It goes like that . . . phoom!'

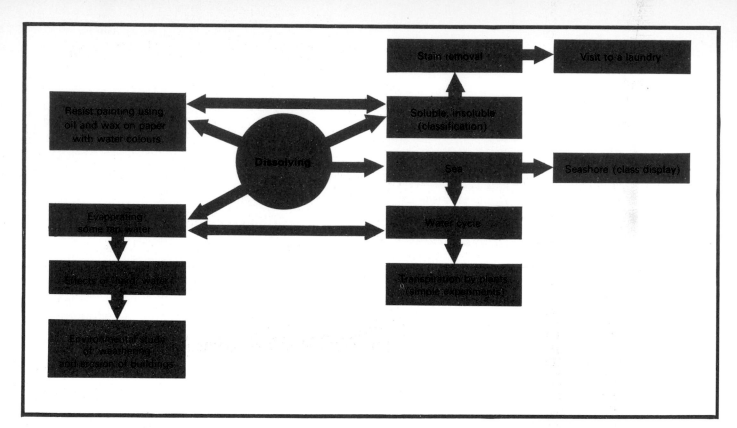

Which of the words in the list on page 20 will most help children to form concepts? This may depend on whether they can use the words in many different situations. For example, consider the flexibility of the words 'repel', 'mix', 'transparent', 'wax', 'porous'.

> Do you consciously introduce new words? Do you help children to use their own resources of words?
>
> Tape-recordings might help here.

Activities

1 Consider the list of concepts on page 20. Construct an activity around each word. With resource material such as Science 5/13 books it is possible to provide experiences that will reinforce the formation of concepts from resist painting (see bibliography: 8, 9, 10). For example:

Repelling	Magnets
	Electricity
Dissolving	Soluble, insoluble substances
	Stain removal
	Sea water
Porosity	Soil
	Building materials
Transparency Opacity	The effects of light

2 Make your own plans for developing a topic. Discuss these and get the children's ideas. You could start with a question like 'What other things repel, dissolve, etc?'

3 Make a record, perhaps a flow diagram (see above), of how the children's investigations actually developed.

3 Working with powder colour and inks

You will need:

Powder colours (from which to make liquid paint)
Washable inks
Containers
Water
Straws and other tubes with different diameters
Droppers
Stiff bristle brushes
White paper

Trying it yourself

Powder colour and inks can be applied in several different ways. Try the following with any variations you wish. Wet paper produces different effects from dry paper.

Drop liquid colours onto the paper which you then move so that the drops run and sometimes trickle into each other.

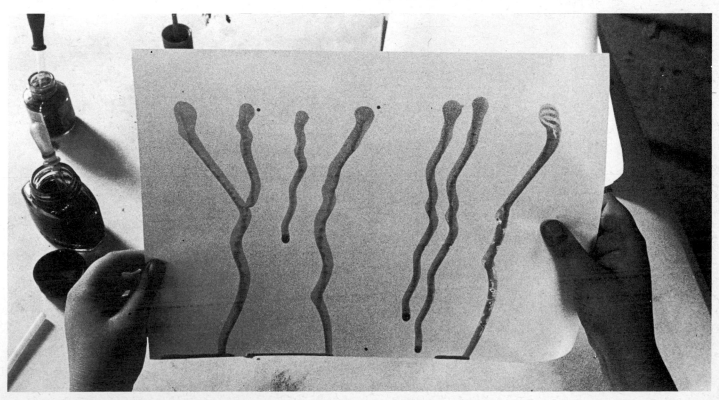

Drop liquid colours from various heights onto the paper.

Drop liquid colours onto paper and, as well as letting them run, puff them with a milk straw (see page 15 top).

Spatter colours onto paper using a stiff bristle brush (see page 14 right).

Investigate the effects of applying paints and inks in different ways, not only with brush, roller or dropper. Try sticks, hair, cottonwool, sponges, wishbones, pieces of card and string (see page 15 bottom).

Analysing your work

Drop, run, puff and spatter painting with colours can be exciting, not only for the pleasing effects that can be produced quite easily, but also for the discovery and surprise entailed in the work.

Observing In producing your paintings did you *observe* what was happening when you used a technique? What you observe depends not only upon the evidence of the senses but upon age and experience. Observation may also depend upon whether you can identify in words or in pictures what you see.

Grouping Did you *group* your observations together? For example, did you bring together in your mind all the different ways of producing spatter effects?

Measuring Did you attempt to *measure*—albeit simply? For example, when you trickled paint did you attempt to gauge the amount needed for specific runs?

When you mixed powder colour, did you vary the amount of water to achieve a suitable consistency? Did you vary the height from which you dropped paint or the angle of the paper when you made it run?

Experimenting Did you *experiment* at all? Putting together the processes on page 23 and those on this page, did you have an *idea* and then try to work out a test under conditions that you *controlled*, that is, by changing only *one* variable at a time?

Children's scientific skills

Observing, grouping, measuring and experimenting are well worth developing in yourself and the children since they are important scientific skills by which knowledge is gained.

Children working with powder colour and inks may employ these scientific skills. It depends largely upon how old they are, their ability and their motivation.

24

In the example here how far did Ivor and Suzanne go in observing, grouping, measuring and experimenting?

Ivor and Suzanne, aged ten, described their investigations of puff painting techniques. Notice how many different methods they discovered.

Teacher: 'What methods are you using, Suzanne?'
Suzanne: 'A flat and a straight up [blowing with the straw held horizontally and vertically].'
Teacher: 'Blowing down into it where it's deep or shallow—or what?'
Suzanne: 'Where it's deep.'

Teacher: 'What does that do?'
Suzanne: 'Sprays.'
Teacher: 'And when you blow along it?'
Suzanne: 'Makes it go all spidery.'
Teacher: 'What methods did you use, Ivor?'
Ivor: 'Horizontally—and putting it over the top of it so it sprays everywhere. And . . . er, sort of blowing it along.'
Teacher: 'I see you tried that wide tube as well as the straw, Ivor. Which is best?'
Ivor: 'The narrow tube.'
Teacher: 'Why?'
Ivor: 'With the big one it seems to push it everywhere. It makes bigger lines instead of small ones.'
Teacher: 'But isn't there a difference when you blow harder?'

Ivor: 'Blowing *hard* with this [the wide tube] it seems to push it everywhere and make thin lines. Blowing ordinary it makes fat lines.'
Teacher: 'What happened when you used the shiny paper?'
Ivor: 'Well, it went a bit lighter on it.'

How might you introduce drop, run, puff and spatter painting in order to encourage the application of scientific skills? What might you be looking for as children work so that you can help them develop scientific skills? Record what actually happened.

More things to do

Here is a list of further activities. You may wish to try them, and then consider:

Which scientific skills each one might foster.
How you could organize each one.

Mixing colours
1   How many different colours can be made from combinations of red, blue and yellow?

2   Can you make these colours from any others?

3   How many shades of the same colour can you make?

4   What is the effect of *black* and *white* on colours?

5   Is there a way of ensuring that the same colour is produced each time two or more colours are mixed?

Information about colour mixing can be found in *The Rays of Light* by L. Basford and J. Pick, and in many science textbooks.

See bibliography: 12, and page 16 right.

Separating colours
1   Mix together small quantities of water-soluble inks and/or food colourings. Put a spot of a mixture onto a sheet of blotting paper and let it dry. Put another spot in the same place; let this dry and continue until you have built up a concentrated dry spot of colour. Add plain water to the spot a drop at a time (page 16 left).

2   Suspend a piece of blotting paper in a mixture of inks and food colourings, diluted with an equal quantity of water. What happens next is due to the different rates at which different pigments move through the porous paper. In a refined form the technique is known as chromatography and can be used to separate mixtures.

3   Look carefully with a magnifying glass at a picture from a colour magazine. Is it possible to build up pictures using small dots of colour applied with a brush or biro?

Here is another type of problem. Can colours be grouped into classes, say 'hot' and 'cold', 'happy' and 'sad', 'rainy' and 'sunny'?

What does the picture below suggest to you?

Blowing bubbles to find rainbow colours

Separating colours from mixtures of washable inks and food colourings

Bibliography

For direct work with children

1 Ash, Beryl, and Dyson, Anthony (1970) *Introducing Dyeing and Printing*. Batsford. Clear descriptive accounts of simple classroom techniques.

2 Busby, R. J. (1969) *Beginner's Guide to Brass Rubbing*. Pelham Books. This book with nos 3, 6, 9 provides a basis for the kind of topic work to which paints and rubbings could well be linked.

3 Fletcher, Edward (1972) *Bottle Collecting*. Blandford Press.

4 Kampmann, Lothar (1973) *Found by Chance*. Evans Bros.

5 Kampmann, Lothar (1968) *Pictures with Paints*. Batsford.

Books nos 4 and 5 are full of useful suggestions with good colour illustrations; the approach is very much to develop techniques through experiment.

6 Lindley, K. A. (1965) *Of Graves and Epitaphs*. Hutchinson.

7 Pluckrose, Henry (1969) *The Art and Craft Book*. Evans Bros. A useful general guide to classroom art techniques, and a resource for many of the techniques suggested in this book.

8 Schools Council Science 5/13 (1973) *Coloured things*, Stages 1 and 2. Macdonald Educational. A wealth of suggestions and extensions of direct relevance to this book.

9 Schools Council Science 5/13 (1973) *Trees*, Stages 1 and 2. Macdonald Educational.

10 Schools Council Science 5/13 (1972) *With objectives in mind*. Macdonald Educational. One of the few available books linking curriculum objectives with practice.

11 Skinner, Michael Kingley (1973) *How to Make Rubbings*. Studio Vista. Includes descriptions of the use of rubbing techniques on ironwork, brasses and many other types of surface.

For further information and ideas

12   Basford, L. and Pick, J. (1966) *The Rays of Light*. Foundation of Optics, Foundations of Science Library. Sampson Low, Marston & Co.

13   Brady, Charles (1970) 'Science Teaching and the Development of Scientific Concepts in Children'. School Science Review, 51, No. 177, pages 765–770. An introductory account with bibliography.

14   Britton, James (1971) *Language and Learning*. Allen Lane (now Longman). A useful book by an authority on language use.

15   Rosen, Connie and Harold (1973) *The Language of Primary School Children*. Penguin. Contains a large collection of material gathered as part of the work of the Schools Council Project on Language Development in the Primary School. Read particularly pages 64–65.

Acknowledgements

The author and publishers gratefully acknowledge the help given by:

The staff and children of:

Brookfield County Primary Junior School, Larkfield, Kent
Sherbrooke Primary Infants and Junior School, London SW6
Wrotham Primary School, Wrotham, Kent

Students and science technicians of Philippa Fawcett College of Education, London SW16

Nicola Dewji, B.Ed.
Tony Dyson, Head of Art Department, Philippa Fawcett College of Education
Janet Moffat, B.Ed.

Illustration credits
Photographs
Kevin Morgan, page 27
Terry Williams, all other photographs

Line drawings by GWA Design Consultants

Cover design by GWA Design Consultants